INNOVATORS
TACKLING THE
ENERGY CRISIS

Robyn Hardyman

LUCENT
PRESS

Published in 2020 by
Lucent Press, an Imprint of Greenhaven Publishing, LLC
353 3rd Avenue
Suite 255
New York, NY 10010

Produced for Lucent by Calcium
Designer: Paul Myerscough
Picture researcher: Rachel Blount
Editors: Sarah Eason and Jennifer Sanderson

Picture credits: Cover: Shutterstock: ssuaphotos; Inside: Altarock: pp. 26, 27; AW Energy: p. 19; Eco Wave Power: pp. 1l, 20, 21; Epoch Microchips (Pty) Ltd: p. 39; Equinor: p. 11; Indoor Reality Inc.: pp. 1cl, 9; Minesto: p. 18; Oxford PV: pp. 1cr, 36, 37; Plant-e: pp. 1r, 42, 43; PowerFilm Solar: pp. 32, 33; Shutterstock: Anette Andersen: p. 25; BrianPlrwin: pp. 3, 28; M. Cornelius: p. 29; Andrea Danti: p. 44; Zhu Difeng: p. 7; lafoto: p. 14; Kefca: p. 5; Kodda: p. 4; Jos Macouzet: p. 24; Bruce MacQueen: p. 12; MaxyM: p. 15; Monkey Business Images: p. 41; Pi-Lens: p. 6; Andrey Polivanov: p 16; Roschetzky Photography: p. 35; SasinTipchai: p. 8; Danila Shtantsov: p. 45; Sirtravelalot: p. 30; Joseph Sohm: p. 10; Johan Swanepoel: p. 22; TAW4: p. 38; Vvoe: p. 34; Bildagentur Zoonar GmbH: p. 40; Solar Roadways: Sam Cornett: p. 31; Wikimedia commons: P123: p. 17; Stepheng3: p. 23; X team: p. 13.

Cataloging-in-Publication Data

Names: Hardyman, Robyn.
Title: Innovators tackling the energy crisis / Robyn Hardyman.
Description: New York : Lucent Press, 2020. | Series: Earth's innovators | Includes glossary and index.
Identifiers: ISBN 9781534565456 (pbk.) | ISBN 9781534565463 (library bound) | ISBN 9781534565470 (ebook)
Subjects: LCSH: Environmental engineering--Juvenile literature. | Green technology--Juvenile literature. | Sustainable engineering--Juvenile literature. | Energy conservation--Juvenile literature. | Renewable energy sources--Juvenile literature.
Classification: LCC TA170.H37 2020 | DDC 628--dc23

Printed in the United States of America

CPSIA compliance information: Batch #BS19KL:
For further information, contact Greenhaven Publishing, LLC, New York, New York, at 1-844-317-7404.

Please visit our website, www.greenhavenpublishing.com.
For a free color catalog of all our high-quality books, call toll free 1-844-317-7404 or fax 1-844-317-7405.

Contents

CHAPTER 1

A WORLD OF ENERGY

One of the biggest challenges facing the world today is how to meet the growing need for energy in a sustainable way. The world's population has doubled in the last 50 years to about 7.6 billion, and industrialization is growing in developing countries. To sustain our modern lives, we need to change the ways we power our world.

The Problem with Fossil Fuels

More than half of our energy comes from burning fossil fuels, such as coal, oil, and natural gas, which we extract from the ground. However, our ever increasing use of these fuels is having a devastating effect on the planet. Burning fossil fuels creates gases that warm our atmosphere, contributing to climate change. Scientists tell us we must urgently reduce our use of energy sources that create harmful emissions. But how can we ensure the lights stay on?

Our dependence on burning fossil fuels for our energy is harming the planet and is not sustainable.

A Developing Demand

The rapid economic development in Africa, Latin America, and Asia is an important part of the energy problem. Energy consumption in these places has been lower than in the developed world, but as these economies grow and their people expect a higher standard of living, their energy use is about to significantly increase. Many of these regions have hot climates, and scientists believe that the demand for energy for cooling is soon going to be an even greater challenge than for heating.

Innovators around the world are using their science, technology, engineering, and math (STEM) skills, their creativity, and their drive to come up with solutions to this truly global problem. And we can all play a part in the solution by reducing our energy use and choosing sustainable sources where we can. A challenge on this scale, however, needs inspired individuals, researchers, businesses, and governments to work together.

Renewable Energy

Innovators are working on ways to deliver cleaner energy from renewable sources. These are all around us: the sun, the wind, the oceans, and the heat in the ground beneath our feet. Innovators are creating small-scale projects in their local communities, they are pushing the boundaries of our knowledge in research labs, and they are working to influence governments and big business around the world. Already about one-fifth of the world's energy comes from renewable sources, but there is still a long way to go.

Air-conditioning units, like these outside apartments in Hong Kong, use a lot of energy.

air-conditioning units

How We Use Energy

A very important part of the challenge of solving the world's energy problem is to control the amount of energy people consume. We use energy all the time, usually in the form of electricity from a power station, when we switch on the lights, the television, a computer, or a refrigerator.

Smart Meters

Most of us are unaware of how much electricity we use and how much we waste. A meter in our home measures the units of electricity we use, to figure out the cost. One recent innovation is the smart meter. This monitors the amount of electricity being used in real time, with a display showing users the amount and the cost of that electricity. Knowing this helps households control their electricity usage, and perhaps adjust it to use more during times when the cost is lower and less at other times.

By 2016, U.S. electric utilities had installed about 70.8 million smart meters, and more than 85 percent of those were in households. Smart meters are now in almost 50 percent of U.S. homes, recording

Smart meters allow us to see how much energy we are using, so we can cut down and save money.

electricity usage every hour and feeding that information back to the utility provider. When we are aware of how we are using electricity and how much it costs, we are more likely to reduce our consumption. The utility companies benefit, too. They learn at what times demand is highest and can adjust their supply to meet that demand.

Smart Grids

Electricity is delivered to us through a grid from a power station to the cables in our homes. Traditionally, this system has been inefficient and unreliable. New smart grid technology is leading the way in improving this by reacting quickly to change energy supply to match changes in demand. By doing so, a smart grid can reduce emissions from greenhouse gases.

Many businesses are investing in smart-grid technology, so experts think that, by 2020, this sector will be worth more than $400 billion. One day soon, the electric devices in our homes, such as washing machines and dishwashers, will also be "smart." They will be able to figure out when the power supply is cheapest, then turn themselves on at the most suitable times, based on the preferences the user sets.

INGENIOUS INNOVATIONS

Home energy monitors are a recent innovation. Wired into your home's electrical panel, they gather information on how much electricity is being used by your electrical appliances, heating or cooling, and lights. Now you can examine your house's environmental impact and take action to improve it.

In this smart home, all the heating, cooling, and electrical appliances can be monitored with one device.

Indoor Reality

One of the main ways that buildings waste energy is through bad design. Things such as windows that do not close properly, doors left open, and walls and roofs lacking insulation all let expensively generated heat escape from a home or an office.

In our modern, energy-conscious world, we cannot afford to waste our energy in this way. It is expensive for the person paying for the energy and expensive for the health of the planet. One innovator decided to address this problem. She is Avideh Zahkor, a professor of engineering at the University of California, Berkeley. Zahkor and her team have come up with a system for quickly mapping energy use throughout a building. The system is lightweight and portable, and is carried inside a backpack by a person who walks through the building to be scanned. Zahkor's device is called the Indoor Reality Pack. As well as mapping the ways that energy is lost around a building, it can also show ways to reduce that unnecessary energy loss through improved design.

Large spaces, such as this warehouse, are perfect locations for using the Indoor Reality Pack to improve their energy efficiency.

Walk-Through Design

The Indoor Reality Pack consists of a collection of cameras and sensors. As the person wearing it walks through the building, these make three-dimensional (3-D) "heat maps" of the space, showing the temperature throughout. This exciting new technology works quickly, too. The pack can complete a scan of a 69,000-square-foot (6,410 sq m) building in about one-sixth of the time needed to do the same job by hand. Another major advantage is that the pack can go wherever a person can walk, so it can cover areas such as staircases, uneven surfaces, and attics, which are hard for other systems to access.

Many people can benefit from using this energy-saving technology, including engineers and architects designing buildings and their interiors, construction firms building them, and real estate professionals marketing them. One engineer commented, "Few energy engineers have opportunities to work with game-changing engineering tools—but I did when I used Indoor Reality's handheld and backpack data acquisition systems ... The virtual walkthrough and annotation features allowed me to 'revisit' the mechanical rooms, again and again, and come up with energy-saving ideas that I might otherwise have missed."

The Indoor Reality Pack is comfortable to wear and easy to use. Its batteries last for up to four hours.

CHAPTER 2

WIND POWER

Almost everywhere in the world, you can feel the wind on your face. It may be a breeze just light enough to rustle the leaves, or it may be a gale that almost blows you over. Whatever its size, this movement of the air contains energy. We are developing ways to harness that energy and use it to power our world.

Turning Blades

To make electricity from the wind, you need to use its power to turn the blades of large windmills, called wind turbines. The turning blades are connected to a turbine inside the structure, which generates electricity that can then be stored. One wind turbine will not create much electricity, so turbines are usually grouped together on wind farms.

John Dabiri, a scientist at Stanford University, had an innovative idea about how to group smaller 30-foot (9 m) wind turbines. These ones have blades that turn like a spinning top. He noticed that fish move most easily in the water when they are grouped in schools. Arranging the smaller turbines in a pattern more like the diamond shape that swimming fish form would make far more efficient use of available land.

These wind turbines that spin around like a top are shorter than standard turbines, so they have less impact on the landscape.

Floating wind farms, such as Hywind off the coast of Scotland, can be used farther out to sea than anchored turbines.

Offshore Wind

Wind turbines must be located in windy places. These may be on land, often in elevated locations, or offshore, out at sea. Some people think that turbines spoil the landscape, so offshore wind farms are a popular choice. However, fixing turbines to the seafloor can be a challenge. The first commercial wind farm to use floating turbines far out at sea is Hywind, off the coast of Scotland, United Kingdom (U.K.). Hywind started to deliver electricity at the end of 2017, powering about 20,000 homes. This is an exciting development because being able to site wind farms far out in deep seas opens up many more possible locations. There are plans for similar projects in the United States, Norway, Portugal, and Japan.

INGENIOUS INNOVATIONS

Wind turbines kill birds, possibly more than 300,000 each year in the United States alone. The U.S. National Wind Technology Center (NWTC) is working to detect endangered birds, such as eagles, as they approach the turbines, so the blades can be stopped. The blades are mounted with scanners or camera detectors. So far, the system seems to be working. More than 90 percent of the eagles that were used to test the system were detected within 1.2 miles (2 km) of the turbines.

Making Wind Power Pay

The cost of creating energy from the wind has fallen a lot over the last decade, but wind power is still an expensive choice. New innovations are emerging all the time to make wind power more affordable, so that this renewable resource and this brilliant technology can be used as part of our sustainable future.

Massive Investment

In the United States, New York State is leading a research and development hub dedicated to developing offshore wind energy for the whole country. The United States Department of Energy (DOE) is spending millions of dollars over the next few years to support researchers and industries, so they can collaborate on finding ways to cut the costs of this technology. The aim of the work is to allow wind power to make a significant contribution to the country's renewable energy program.

As the U.S. government spends more on developing wind power, we may see more turbines, such as these along the Lake Erie shoreline near Buffalo, New York.

Reaching New Heights

The higher up you travel, the stronger the wind becomes. Building wind turbines that are hundreds of feet tall, however, is very expensive. Some people also do not like the way they look.

A California company, Makani, is looking at ways around this problem. Makani is building giant "kites" that are tethered to the ground but take off into the skies with wind turbines fixed to them. The kites can soar up to 984 feet (300 m), which is around 328 feet (100 m) higher than the world's tallest turbine tower. As the kites soar in huge circles, the turbines capture the wind's energy and pass it to the ground through an electrical cable within the tethers.

long wing

wind turbine

tail

The Makani kite is transported to a site in California for an important testing session.

A Mix of Solutions

Another way to make wind power pay is to mix it with other technologies. One remarkable innovator in Germany, Ursula Sladek, has created the world's first cooperatively owned renewable power company: EWS. Sladek, a local schoolteacher, wanted to reduce the dependence of her local area on nuclear energy. She and a few supporters campaigned to raise the money to take over their local power grid, bringing energy ownership back to the community. Twenty years later, EWS uses energy generated by wind, the sun, and water to power more than 100,000 homes and businesses. The German government is now in agreement with Sladek's goal of creating 100 percent of the country's power from renewable sources by 2050.

Capture Mobility

You never know when a brilliant idea is going to come. The difficult part is to realize it is brilliant, and to work on putting it into action. Pakistani electrical engineer Sanwal Muneer had his moment of brilliance when he was standing next to a racetrack in Malaysia. As the cars sped by, the wind they created whooshed past him. This made Muneer wonder if roadside turbines could capture that wind and turn it into usable energy.

Muneer set out to design a turbine that could do the job. As his ideas began to develop, he realized that he needed a team, so he set up a company called Capture Mobility. The turbine he designed is shaped like a twisted helix. Placed along a highway, an airport runway, or a subway track, lines of these turbines convert the wind into energy. Each one is also topped with a solar panel to add to the power generated. Roadsides can be very polluted places, so the turbines also contain a removable filter that absorbs the pollutants the traffic creates, making the air cleaner.

It is not just race cars that create wind as they drive fast. The wind created by cars on the highway can be turned into electricity, too.

Homes in remote areas without access to the grid could use the Capture Mobility turbines.

Generating Power

It is hard to believe that just one Capture Mobility turbine can create a lot of energy. However, once its battery is fully charged, it can hold enough power to run two lamps and a fan for 40 hours. This power can be sent either to the national grid or to local energy grids. It can then be used to power local communities, perhaps in rural areas along major highways. In fact, these turbines can even be installed on the rooftops of homes in windy, remote areas that are not on the grid, to provide the homes with electricity. A mobile charging port can be connected to them, allowing people to keep devices such as cell phones charged.

As well as providing electricity, Capture Mobility's turbine is an excellent way to reduce the pollution that traffic causes and to bring renewable energy to remote areas. As long as the traffic thunders past, these devices will be making the most of it.

Muneer and Capture Mobility have won many awards, including the United Nations (UN) Clean Energy Award and an Outstanding Achievement award from the U.K. government's Department of Trade and Investment. Muneer's technology has also attracted the backing of Shell, the giant energy company, and is now being tested on a stretch of busy road in Scotland, U.K.

CHAPTER 3

ENERGY FROM THE OCEAN

In the world of renewable energy, harnessing the power of water has often been left behind. Although water covers more than 70 percent of Earth's surface, the cost of designing and installing the technology needed to extract energy from it has been too high.

Difficult but Possible

The ocean can be a hostile place, with enormous waves and hurricane-force winds, and these have brought huge challenges to generating electricity from it. Traditionally, other forms of renewable energy, such as wind and solar power, have been easier to develop. Today, however, when we accept that we need all the energy innovations we can find, there are many exciting developments in the world of extracting energy from the ocean.

Scientists estimate that the energy that could be harvested from the world's oceans is equal to twice the amount of electricity that the world currently produces. Also, two-thirds of the world's population lives within 250 miles (400 km) of a sea coast, and more than half of the population of the United States lives within 50 miles (80 km) of the coast. It makes sense to create electricity close to where people live.

The awesome power of the ocean could be a very valuable source of energy, if we can master the technological challenges it poses.

Waves and Tides

There are two main ways to harness the power of the oceans: wave energy and tidal energy. The ocean is constantly moving. That movement has the potential to generate a lot of electricity. Wave farm devices convert that movement energy, or kinetic energy, into pressure, which spins a generator to produce electricity. The movement of waves is complicated, though. Waves can move up and down or sideways, so it is a challenge to figure out how best to extract energy from them.

Tidal power harnesses the movement of the ocean as the tide takes water in toward the shore and out again, usually twice every 24 hours. Turbines in the water have blades that turn in the current. A tidal barrage is a huge structure, like a dam, where a reservoir fills up as the tide comes in and empties as it goes out. That falling water is used to turn turbines. The technology may be complex, but the ocean energy sector is full of ideas, with hundreds of companies developing an extraordinary array of devices, backed by billions of dollars of investment.

This machine is harnessing the power of waves off the coast of Portugal, in southern Europe.

Tidal Power and Wave Power

The challenge of harnessing the power of the ocean is creating many exciting and innovative ideas around the world. Ocean Energy Systems is a group of 25 nations that have come together to collaborate on advancing the technology for harnessing the power of the ocean.

Underwater Kite

One of the issues with tidal energy is that the speed at which the water moves is quite slow. Swedish business Minesto has developed an underwater power plant shaped like a kite. As it "flies" through the moving water in a figure-eight pattern, the wing pushes a turbine through the water, sweeping a large area at a speed faster than the actual current of the water. This produces much more electricity than it would if the turbine were stationary.

The electricity flows through a cable in the tether that holds the kite to the ocean floor. From there, another cable carries the power to the shore. This exciting new technology is being tested off the coast of Wales, U.K.

The largest planned tidal power project in the world is the MeyGen project. This uses an array of turbines off the coast of Scotland and is already sending power to the grid. A sea channel here, between the coast and a nearby island, speeds up the flow of the current.

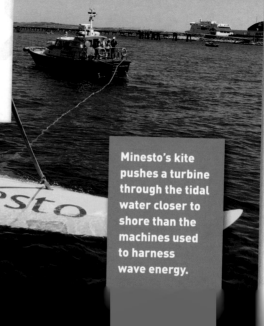

Minesto's kite pushes a turbine through the tidal water closer to shore than the machines used to harness wave energy.

The WaveRoller operates near the shore at 26 to 66 feet (8 to 20 m) deep, where the wave surge is most powerful.

Turbine Design

The design of the turbines is attracting innovation, too. Some have blades that turn to generate power. Some have three blades, while others have four or six. Others use a scoop-shaped rotating structure. Water catches in the scoops to drive the turbine. Another design forces the tidal water through a funnel, where it flows faster, generating power that way. A company called OpenHydro has developed a system of 52-foot (16 m) hoops with inward-pointing blades. This is being used in Canada's Bay of Fundy to generate power.

A Wave of Innovation

Wave power devices are highly innovative, too. Some float on the surface to generate power.

The WaveRoller uses a combination of a wide panel hinged to the ocean floor and a power take-off (PTO) unit. The panel moves back and forth with the waves while the PTO converts the power captured by the panel into electricity.

INGENIOUS INNOVATIONS

Simple wave power devices, called bulge wave converters, are effective at withstanding the power of the ocean. These are a long rubber tube, tethered to the ocean floor. Water enters the tube at one end, and the passing wave causes pressure to build up through the tube. This forces the water through the tube to a turbine at the other end. It is a simple, yet effective, way to ride with the waves to create power.

Eco Wave Power

Inna Braverman is a celebrated innovator and entrepreneur. She founded Eco Wave Power at the age of 24 and has been called one of the most influential young people in the world. Her company has become a world leader in the technology that allows companies to harvest the power of the ocean.

For Braverman, clean energy has been a personal priority. She was born in Ukraine soon after the major disaster in the nuclear power plant there at Chernobyl, in 1986. The disaster released terrible pollution across a wide area. Braverman suffered health problems as a result. Her experience made her determined to find ways to prevent such an accident from happening again, by developing cleaner ways of generating electricity.

Inna Braverman spoke at the opening of Eco Wave Power's first wave power station in Europe, in Gibraltar near Spain.

DO IT LIKE GIBRALTAR

YOUR PLANET

Eco Wave Power's floaters can be attached to any existing structure along the shore, where they move up and down with the waves.

Inexpensive but Effective

Eco Wave Power has developed an inexpensive technology to harvest wave energy. Its wave energy power stations can produce electricity at a lower cost than competing energy generation methods because they use mainly off-the-shelf parts, need little maintenance, and last a long time. The "floaters" are located on or near the shore, attached to structures such as breakwaters, jetties, and floating or fixed platforms.

The floaters move up and down with the waves, and their movement is carried to a shore-based power station, where it is used to power a generator, producing electricity. It is a big advantage having only the floaters and the pistons in the water, with all the other technical equipment on land, where it can easily be accessed and maintained.

After testing different designs for several years, Eco Wave Power has created two devices, the Wave Clapper and the Power Wing, which both have in-built storm-protection mechanisms. The floaters have sensors that can detect when a storm is coming, then adjust the height of the floats to keep them safe, either lowering them completely under the water or raising them.

Braverman's innovation is currently being used along the coast of Gibraltar, near Spain. This is the first wave power station in Europe to be connected to a grid. More projects using Eco Wave Power are in development in China, Mexico, Israel, Chile, and the U.K.

CHAPTER 4

ENERGY FROM THE GROUND

We live on an amazing planet. Most of its surface may be covered with water and the land may feel cool to our touch, but deep underground, Earth is hot. The closer you go toward the core at the center, the hotter it gets. This heat beneath our feet, called geothermal energy, can be used as a constant source of power.

Earth's core is 9,900 degrees Fahrenheit (5,500 degrees C), but it is a very, very long way down. The outer 10 feet (3 m) of Earth's surface stay at a nearly constant 50 to 61 degrees Fahrenheit (10 to 16 degrees C) throughout the year, and that heat is useful to us. We can harness it to heat our buildings and our water directly. A community called Fairwater has been built in Australia, heated and cooled only by geothermal pumps. All the houses are heated and cooled this way, and so is its water.

The natural heat in Earth's ground could be an unlimited source of energy for the world.

How Geothermal Power Works

By drilling down farther, we can convert the intense heat below ground to electricity using geothermal power plants. These use that heat to create steam, which turns a turbine. The turbine drives a generator to produce electricity. The United States is a world leader in producing geothermal electricity and is investing heavily in its research and development. Experts think geothermal power could provide more than 10 percent of the country's energy needs. The largest geothermal plant in the world is in California at the Geysers Geothermal Complex. Here, 22 geothermal power plants draw steam from more than 350 wells.

Innovative Techniques

Generating geothermal power on a large scale brings some challenges, however. Conditions must be just right, with the heat close enough to the surface and the rock suitable for drilling. The task involves working with extreme temperatures and pressure. These factors make geothermal power expensive. Innovators are working to address these challenges by developing new drilling techniques.

In June 2018, the United States DOE announced $140 million in funding for a new center of geothermal research and development in Utah. There, a new field laboratory will conduct experiments on new ways to develop geothermal power. Scientists at the center will work on creating man-made underground reservoirs of very hot water, so that geothermal power can be produced in places where the perfect conditions do not occur naturally. This creative innovation is an important part of the country's work in developing renewable energy sources.

Geothermal power stations like this one in Sonoma, California, are located in open country, as they use a lot of land for their operation.

Heat Beneath Our Feet

Geothermal power plants like this one in Mexico could soon be a common sight in Latin America.

Around the world, governments and businesses are investing in developing geothermal power. This is a very expensive process, so the innovations must be paid for by the big players. Collaboration between researchers and industries is producing some promising results.

Latin America

Experts think that there is great potential for geothermal power in Latin America. With underground reservoirs of hot water, the natural conditions are right there.

The region is also in need of affordable and clean energy. Mexico was the first country in the region to develop geothermal power, and is now the fourth biggest producer in the world after the United States, the Philippines, and Indonesia. It aims to meet 35 percent of its energy needs with geothermal power by 2024. Costa Rica has been developing geothermal power for some time, too.

Volcano Power

The small country of Iceland is a world leader in its use of geothermal energy, and has six geothermal power plants. Now, there are plans for this country to develop geothermal power in a new way so that it can send its electricity across northern Europe. At the moment, Iceland's geothermal plants drill thousands of feet underground to natural reservoirs of hot, pressurized water. The new technique will try to harness the power of the local volcanoes.

Scientists plan to drill into a lake of molten magma in one volcano. They will then pump water through the boiling lake, in a pipeline. The water will be heated, creating steam that will be used to power turbines to create electricity. The electricity can then be sent by undersea cables to countries such as the Netherlands, Denmark, and the U.K.

Iceland has many volcanoes like this one, each with lakes of molten rock beneath them that can be used to heat water and create steam.

INGENIOUS INNOVATIONS

Drilling through hard rock is challenging, so companies with experience drilling in oil fields are using their expertise to develop new drilling technologies. One has recently successfully demonstrated an advanced drilling system designed for the conditions of geothermal power. It uses a very temperature-resistant lubricant in the drilling fluid to cope with the high temperatures underground, a drill made of the strongest metal, and an extremely powerful motor that can work the drill for many hours, to reach far underground.

AltaRock Energy

Susan Petty is a geothermal engineer and an extraordinary innovator in the area of geothermal power. She is the founder of AltaRock Energy, a company that has developed a new process that offers a breakthrough in tapping Earth's heat for energy.

The problem with expanding the use of geothermal energy is that natural underground reservoirs of heated water do not occur in many places. In the United States, for example, they are much more common in western areas than elsewhere in the country. Studies have shown, however, that there is enough recoverable energy in the hot rocks of the entire United States to supply a large portion of the total power consumption. AltaRock has developed new technology to improve the efficiency and sustainability of Enhanced Geothermic Systems (EGS), which will make it possible to generate geothermal power in many more locations.

Susan Petty (right) is an innovator who has spent her career developing geothermal power.

Tests must be conducted on the ground before work can start on the drilling and pumping process.

EGS involves pumping water into naturally occurring cracks in the ground, 2 to 3 miles (3 to 5 km) below the surface. The water opens up the cracks slightly, so that artificial underground reservoirs are created. There, the natural heat of Earth heats the water to around 600 degrees Fahrenheit (300 degrees C). The hot water and the steam that are also created are then pumped back to the surface to a power plant. Here, the steam is used to turn turbines that produce electricity. The hot water is cooled and sent underground to start the process over again. This closed system, which recycles the water, also ensures that water is not wasted.

Growing the Business

Susan Petty studied geology at Princeton University, and groundwater hydrology at the University of Hawaii. She founded AltaRock in 2007. Since then, she has grown the business and raised more than $50 million in funding for research and development projects from businesses and the DOE. AltaRock is conducting surveys in many areas across the United States, to look for suitable locations for expanding existing geothermal power plants and for creating entirely new ones.

This new technology has the potential to make geothermal power possible in more locations and less expensive to develop. That would mean that it can join wind and solar power as a major contributor to the world of renewable energy.

CHAPTER 5

SOLAR ENERGY

Even though the sun is 93 million miles (150 million km) away, in every minute, enough energy from it reaches Earth to meet the whole world's energy needs for a year. Solar power is created using the sun's energy. This comes in two forms: heat (or thermal energy) and light. We can use both of these to meet our increasing need for energy.

Thermal Power

Solar power is the world's fastest growing source of energy. Recent years have seen incredible innovations, as the technology has advanced at lightning speed, making solar power more efficient, more flexible in its uses, and cheaper.

The simplest use of solar power is for heating. In countries with warm climates, devices installed on the roofs of buildings concentrate the heat of the sun to heat water for everyday use. The water is stored in tanks and no electricity is used. Solar heating can also be used for cooking. Millions of people around the world do not have access to electricity and cook over fires fueled by wood or dung. The smoke from these is bad for people's health and pollutes the atmosphere. Innovators have created solar ovens so people who do not have access to electricity can cook cleanly and for free. They can also boil water to make it safe to drink.

Ivanpah Solar Electric Generating System in California is the world's largest thermal solar power station. Sunlight is focused onto boilers, which heat water, on top of three power towers.

Electricity from Sunlight

Sunlight is turned into electricity using solar panels in a process called photovoltaics, or PV. These panels are made using thin wafers of silicon, which absorb the energy in sunlight and turn it into an electric current. One of the biggest benefits of solar power is that it can deliver electricity to places where there is no power grid, such as remote areas and developing countries. Nearly 20 percent of the world's population has no electricity, but innovations in solar power are changing that.

A group of students at Imperial College London, in the U.K., set up BBOXX. The company is taking off-grid energy to the developing world,

delivering PV panels to homes in Rwanda in East Africa. Customers pay a small amount, about the same as they were spending before on kerosene fuel and batteries. Now they have electricity to power lights, phones, and other devices. Life can carry on after dark, including studying to improve young people's education.

Many other innovators are doing similar work in Africa. A German company called Mobisol has installed 85,000 units in Tanzania and Rwanda. Off Grid Electric, based in San Francisco, California, serves 50,000 homes in Tanzania. M-KOPA, a Kenyan company, has provided power to more than 500,000 homes in Kenya, Uganda, and Tanzania.

This simple, solar-powered oven cooks food without creating the harmful smoke that comes from burning wood or coal on an open fire.

Solar Everywhere

Solar power brings electricity to parts of the world that previously had none. It is also replacing fossil-fuel-generated electricity for millions of customers in the developed world. Innovations in solar power are now reaching every aspect of our lives.

Storing the Power

One of the main challenges with solar power is how to store the electricity that PV panels create, so solar power can be kept for use on cloudy days. In 2015, the U.S. electric car company Tesla produced a rechargeable battery, called Powerwall, which has become the most popular choice for residential use. A rapid increase in demand from solar consumers is expected to bring even more efficient and affordable batteries.

A new alternative storage solution is emerging in the form of solar thermal fuel (STF). Professor Jeffrey Grossman of Massachusetts Institute of Technology (MIT) and his team have been developing STFs that store the energy in a battery in a liquid form. The liquid form will be cheaper than traditional batteries.

The solar panels being installed on this roof will bring electricity for the first time to people in a remote area in a developing country.

Solar on the Roof

Some buildings are not suitable for solar panels on their roofs because they do not face the sun. An ingenious innovation is solving this problem. Solar tracking mounts hold PV panels and turn through the day to follow the sun, capturing as much energy as possible. They can even be mounted on the ground.

Some homeowners find the look of solar panels on the roof unsightly. One innovator, Sistine Solar of Boston, Massachusetts, has a solution to this problem: a "solar skin" product that makes it possible for solar panels to match the appearance of a roof, without interfering with the panel's efficiency.

Solar Gardens

Sometimes individuals still cannot install solar panels on their own houses. One innovator in Colorado Springs, Colorado, David Amster-Olszewski, had an idea to help them. He started a company called SunShare, which sets up community solar "gardens." People buy shares in a handful of local panels, and get credit on their utility bill based on how much electricity their panels produce and how much they use. The idea has caught on quickly, and almost 100 projects are now operating in 25 states.

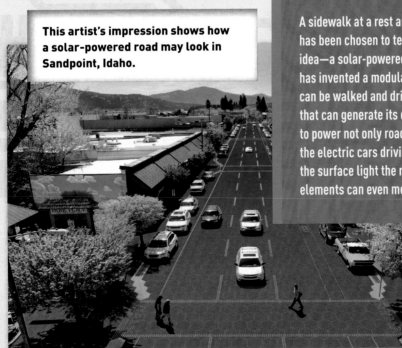

This artist's impression shows how a solar-powered road may look in Sandpoint, Idaho.

INGENIOUS INNOVATIONS

A sidewalk at a rest area along highway Route 66 has been chosen to test an exciting new solar idea—a solar-powered sidewalk. Solar Roadways has invented a modular system of solar panels that can be walked and driven on. Imagine a roadway that can generate its own electricity, and use it to power not only road signs and lights, but also the electric cars driving along it. LED bulbs in the surface light the route at night, and heating elements can even melt snow and ice in winter.

Flexible Solar

Rigid PV panels made up of hundreds of silicon cells have brought a revolution in electricity creation around the world, but they also have their limitations. Innovators in PV have been working to create solar technology that is more flexible. It is literally more flexible, or bendy, and it can be put to many different uses.

Thin Film PV

Another kind of PV material is made using different components from traditional silicon panels. The components are used to create an extremely thin, flexible PV layer. The beauty of this is that it can be attached to other materials, such as metal, plastic, or glass.

These thin film layers weigh much less than conventional PV panels, and they cost less to produce, too. Another advantage is that they work well in cloudy conditions, better than traditional panels do. Also, because they are flexible, they can be used in less conventional, more challenging locations. They can be attached to construction panels or to glass to cover a building in solar power potential. Some new buildings are being designed to be covered in thin film PV panels that blend in well with the other construction materials.

This thin film solar panel can be clipped onto this electric golf cart, to give it power for driving around the course.

The disadvantages of thin film PV, however, are that it is less effective at turning the energy in sunlight into power. You need to cover a larger area of a building to generate the same amount of electricity. Thin film PV also does not last as long, so it has to be replaced more often.

Wearable Solar

People have been wearing solar-powered watches and other gadgets for years, but these all used a hard, plastic material. Two innovators have been working to change all that.

Textile designer Marianne Fairbanks and chemist Tricia Andrew, both from the University of Wisconsin, have invented a way of weaving solar cells into a fabric. Now you could wear a solar shirt! Solar fabric could be used almost anywhere to generate electricity, such as drapes in the home to catch the sunlight through windows, or on seats in the car to make the most of a sunny day. It could be used by the military, or to supply power in refugee camps, or for medical emergencies. The future looks exciting for this creative innovation.

This flexible, portable solar panel can charge while the user is hiking, to provide power for after dark.

Perovskite

The cost of producing solar power has fallen massively in the last decade. Experts say it fell by more than 85 percent between 2009 and 2017. This is because the technology improved rapidly, and more and more people decided to buy it, making the overall costs lower. The challenge remains, however, for solar power to be able to meet our growing energy needs. Expert innovators are forever looking at ways to make solar panels better at turning sunlight into the energy we need.

It is called perovskite. Perovskite behaves differently from silicon in sunlight. All light energy takes the form of waves, and different kinds of light have different wavelengths. Perovskite captures energy from a different part of the wavelength of sunlight from silicon. Researchers have found that this makes it better at converting the light energy into power. A silicon solar cell converts 21 to 22 percent of sunlight into energy. With perovskite, that could rise to more than 30 percent.

Extracting the Sun's Energy

A mineral that is in plentiful supply around the world is emerging as the leader in this race for better PV materials.

Perovskite is a mineral that occurs naturally in the ground. It contains two metals called calcium and titanium.

Silicon is likely to remain the choice of material for making the panels for large-scale solar power farms like this one outside Austin, Texas.

Solar Buildings

Perovskite can be used in a different way from silicon, too. It does not have to be made into rigid PV panels. Instead, it can be used to make a thin solar coating, which can be put on large rolls and used to cover wide areas. Artur Kupczunas is cofounder of a Poland-based perovskite firm called Saule Technologies, and he is excited about the possibilities of perovskite. He believes perovskite could be incorporated into the fabric of new buildings, both in the walls and as windows of the buildings, because the mineral can be made semitransparent. Silicon is too heavy to do that.

Scientists agree that the potential for perovskite is huge, and it is clearly a hot topic of the moment. Nearly 4,000 scientific papers were published on it in 2017 alone. Although experts think that silicon is likely to remain the favored choice of material for large-scale solar farms, perovskite may be the new choice for smaller, constrained spaces, such as homes and schools. Perovskite may also be used in PV systems out in space, which are used to power satellites and other spacecraft. In space, the material's lightness and efficiency would be a big advantage.

Oxford PV

Professor Henry Snaith of Oxford University, U.K., is the leading researcher behind a world-class business that is leading the development of perovskite as a major new material for generating solar power.

Using Perovskite

Professor Snaith began looking at perovskite in the lab in 2009, but he was only looking for a material that could replace the dye in existing solar cells. He was not looking for a new material that could generate the electricity. In 2012, he and his team made the big breakthrough when they realized that perovskite was itself more efficient at turning sunlight into energy than the silicon in traditional PV cells. He knew he had discovered something of major importance, with really exciting opportunities. The method of making the cells was better, too. PV cells could be made with a simple stack of thin layers of perovskite. This was quicker and cheaper than making silicon cells.

New perovskite cells are being tested in the Oxford PV research lab.

Oxford PV

Professor Snaith set up a company called Oxford PV, to work in the U.K. and Germany on developing the potential of his discovery. The company's idea is to combine perovskite with silicon, because great advances have been made in the past decade in making standard solar cells, so it makes sense to use these advances and build on them. Oxford PV's work is now creating solar cells that can extract more than 25 percent of the energy in sunlight, more than has ever been possible before. In June 2018, they broke the world record, with a solar cell extracting 27.3 percent of the energy in sunlight. What is more, they think there is further room for improvement, and that the technology has the potential to reach 33 percent. Oxford PV is developing products to be used on buildings, too.

The importance of Snaith's work has been widely recognized around the world. *Nature* magazine has declared him one of the ten most important people worldwide in all of science, and in 2017, he was named a Clarivate Citation Laureate. This is a list of scientists whose exceptional work makes them likely in the future to be awarded the highest honor in science, a Nobel Prize. The use of perovskite is an incredibly exciting development in the use of solar power as a low-cost, renewable source of energy for our future.

Professor Henry Snaith and his team at Oxford University are leading the research into making perovskite solar cells even better at turning sunlight into electricity.

CHAPTER 6

FINDING NEW SOLUTIONS

Scientists think that by 2040 the world's energy consumption will have increased by almost 50 percent from 2017 levels. This is because developing countries are becoming more industrialized and using more energy to heat and cool their homes, run lights and appliances, and power vehicles. Today, only about one-fifth of the world's energy comes from renewable sources. We need to find more ways to create and deliver the power we are going to need.

Supergrids

One of the problems with having many sources of electricity flow into a power grid is that the supply is not steady and reliable. For example, solar-powered electricity pours in during the day, while wind power flows in when it is windy. These times may not be the same as the times of peak demand for electricity from homes and businesses. Coal-fired or oil-fired power stations are more steady and reliable in their supply.

Innovators are looking at ways for the regions of the world to share their electricity more widely with their neighbors.

Our old grids are not good at coping with this variation. One solution is to make the grids that distribute the electricity bigger. If they receive power from a larger area, there is more chance that the sun will be shining or the wind will be blowing somewhere in that area when demand is high. "Supergrids" are being discussed. These would share supply between several countries, or cover a whole country such as the United States. The U.K. is building underwater connections to the energy grids of countries in northern Europe. There is talk of an Asian supergrid connecting Japan, China, Russia, Mongolia, and South Korea.

Think Small

As well as these very big projects, individuals around the world are working on small-scale solutions to our energy problems. They have bright ideas for generating electricity that can benefit their own community or country. Two such young innovators are Jessica Matthews and Julie Silverman of the United States, who invented a soccer ball that harnesses and stores electricity from play. As players kick the ball, a small generator inside produces electricity. This is stored inside and can later be used to power devices such as lights.

Shalton Mothwa is a young South African nuclear physicist. He grew up fascinated with physics and always wanted to know how things work. After his graduate degree in applied physics, he started looking into the possibility of turning radio signals into electrical energy. Once he had worked that out, he developed the idea of storing that energy in a device called the Aeon Power Bag. This portable bag can be used to charge a cell phone, tablet, or laptop wirelessly, anywhere. The Power Bag offers people in rural areas with no access to electricity the opportunity to be connected.

Shalton Mothwa received financial support to develop his Aeon Power Bag from organizations wanting to support creative innovators.

Innovative Fuels

Our need for fuel shows no signs of reducing, so we need to find ways to make new, more sustainable ones. Innovators both large and small are exploring some original ideas to make this happen.

Biofuels

Biofuels are fuels made from renewable or sustainable sources, such as plants. They can be blended into gasoline or diesel to make them greener by reducing the amount of harmful greenhouse gases they produce. Most biofuels today are produced from corn or sugarcane. The energy giant Shell works with Raizen, a company in Brazil, to produce biofuel from sugarcane. This fuel has 70 percent fewer emissions than gasoline. In Thailand, Shell works with producers of palm oil to make biodiesel.

Fuel from the Kitchen

Cooking oils used for frying are another potential source of fuel. A company in China, MotionEco, is working to transform some of the millions of tons of used cooking oil from restaurants around the country into sustainable biofuel. The biofuel is blended with normal gasoline or diesel, then used for transportation. It is a win-win situation, reducing the amount of greenhouse gases gasoline produces and using a waste product that would otherwise cause pollution when it was thrown away.

Biofuels have an important part to play in replacing the polluting fuels that currently power our cars.

INGENIOUS INNOVATIONS

Arthur Kay is a British innovator who has developed a way to create energy from a common, everyday resource: coffee grounds. He noticed that his unfinished cold coffee had a thin oily film on top of it, and wondered where it came from. He discovered that there was oil in coffee, and that the energy in that oil can be released by burning it. He set up a company called Bio-Bean to explore the technology, and found that he could convert coffee waste from cafés and restaurants into dense lumps, or pellets. These pellets can be burned to warm ovens or even to heat buildings. Next, Arthur created "logs" for the fireplace made from his coffee waste. Now he is working on his latest project, a biodiesel fuel made using coffee waste, which he wants to use to power buses. What an excellent use of the waste produced by people's obsession with coffee!

Perhaps, one day, coffee shops will all be heated by pellets made from their own coffee waste.

Plant-e

Marjolein Helder was a researcher of environmental technology at Wageningen University in the Netherlands when one of her colleagues developed technology to use plants to create electricity. Helder realized the importance of her colleague's work and set up Plant-e, a dynamic young company with a passion for sustainability and innovation. Her business is dedicated to researching and developing the possibilities of using plants to create electricity. That must surely be the greenest kind of electricity there could be.

A Spark of Nature

As plants grow, they produce organic material. Some of this they use for their growth, but the rest goes back into the soil through their roots. The soil is full of microbes, or tiny living things, that break down that organic material. As they do, they produce something very useful: electrons, which are tiny electrically charged particles. Helder thought this process must have potential for our greener future.

Helder presents her company's innovative ideas for generating electricity from plants.

These plants are part of the Plant-e system that is powering the WiFi at this school in the Netherlands.

Her company has devised technology to collect the electrons and use them as electricity in a Plant Microbial Fuel Cell, which is a type of battery. Plant-e is using this technology to develop products that generate electricity from plants.

Watch It Grow

At the moment, this technology produces quite small amounts of electricity. It is about enough to run a lamp for a few hours. However, there are an incredible number of plants in the world. A technology that uses such a plentiful resource has exciting possibilities. If it were used across a wide area, it could produce a very useful amount of power. It is safe to say this technology certainly has the potential to grow.

Recognition and Reward

The prestigious organization the World Economic Forum brings together leaders from government, business, and research to work on solutions to the big problems faced by the world today. As part of its work, it runs a program called Technology Pioneers. This recognizes young companies from around the world that are involved in the design and use of new technologies, and are poised to have a significant impact on business and society. In 2015, the World Economic Forum named Plant-e one of its Technology Pioneers.

INNOVATORS OF THE FUTURE

Pioneering work will always continue, from individuals, researchers, and businesses, as long as we have global problems to solve. The cutting-edge ideas that today may seem a little bizarre could turn out to be the solutions of tomorrow. We must continue to develop our STEM skills and think creatively to drive the innovations of the future.

The Big Solution

There is one solution to the world's energy problem that beats them all. That is called nuclear fusion. The nucleus is the central part of an atom, or particle of matter. Reactions between the nuclei of different substances can create a lot of energy. Nuclear fusion between the substances called deuterium and tritium can produce 11.3 million times more energy than burning coal.

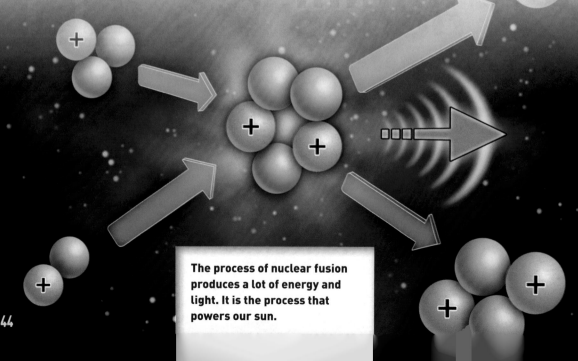

The process of nuclear fusion produces a lot of energy and light. It is the process that powers our sun.

Nuclear fusion does not produce harmful waste products, either. The problem is that we cannot yet get fusion to work well. It needs very, very high temperatures that are millions of degrees Fahrenheit. Scientists have been working on this problem for many years, but there are signs of breakthroughs coming. It will be several decades before we get there, but this could solve all our energy problems.

Powering the Developing World

Meanwhile, others are still innovating. People such as Sohab El Outmani of Morocco are working on ideas to improve the technology of batteries for storing the electricity generated by renewable sources. Ifedayo Oladapo of Nigeria has set up a company called Grit Systems to build a system of smart meters for consumers in his country. In Kenya, Evans Wadongo has set up GreenWize Energy to develop African-designed renewable energy solutions in sub-Saharan Africa. Others are bringing solar power to their rural communities, all so that people in the developing world can have the benefits that access to energy brings.

Windows on the World

Physee is a company in the Netherlands where researchers are developing completely transparent windows that can generate their own electricity. These amazing windows can sense their environment, collect data on it, and use that to decide how to cool, heat, and light the building. They use solar power in an innovative way that looks like an exciting way to make our buildings greener.

Our energy issues are challenging, and there are many hurdles to jump if we are to create an energy-sustainable future. However, the future is looking brighter than ever thanks to the smart ideas of hundreds of innovators around the world. Maybe you will join them one day in helping solve our energy problems through innovative thinking.

The cities of the future will use more renewable sources of energy, to be less wasteful and create a less polluted environment.

Glossary

atmosphere the blanket of gases around Earth

atom the smallest particle of a substance

battery a container in which energy is stored, then converted to electricity when needed

biofuels fuels made from plants and other living things, which are renewable resources

consumption the use of something

current water or air moving in one direction

developing countries poorer countries that are trying to build their economies and improve people's living conditions

emissions the release of something into the environment, particularly of pollution

fossil fuels energy sources, such as coal and oil, that formed over millions of years from the remains of living things in the ground

generator a machine that converts energy into electricity

geology the study of Earth's structure

geothermal the heat beneath Earth's surface

greenhouse gases gases such as carbon dioxide that collect in Earth's atmosphere and trap the sun's heat

grids the networks of cables that distribute electricity from power stations to consumers

hydrology the study of Earth's water

industrialization the process of growing the number of factories in a country to create more wealth

insulation materials that prevent heat loss

lubricant a liquid that helps two materials slide easily over each other

nuclear energy energy that is created by reactions between the nuclei in atoms

organic made of living things

perovskite a mineral in the ground that is being used to create a new kind of solar panel

photovoltaic cell the smallest part of a solar power system, where the sunlight is converted to electricity

photovoltaics (PV) the process of creating electricity from the light of the sun

renewable describes a resource that can be used repeatedly and replaced naturally, such as plants or rainwater

reservoirs large pools of collected water

silicon a natural substance that is used to make one kind of PV cell

sustainable describes a resource that will never run out, such as the sun or wind, or that can be renewed by a natural process, such as planting more seeds

thermal solar power power created using the heat of the sun, rather than its light

turbines machines used to convert the movement of air or a liquid into electricity

utilities electricity, gas, or water provided to homes and businesses

For More Information

Books

Bow, James. *Energy Technology Inspired by Nature*. Mendota Heights, MN: Focus Readers, 2018.

Brearley, Laurie. *Water Power: Energy from Rivers, Waves, and Tides*. New York, NY: Scholastic Children's Press, 2019.

Brundle, Harriet. *Renewable Energy*. New York, NY: KidHaven, 2018.

Dickmann, Nancy. *Using Renewable Energy*. New York, NY: Crabtree Publishing Company, 2019.

Websites

Find out how our energy usage and choices affect the planet at:

www.acespace.org

Discover more about renewable energy sources at:

www.alliantenergykids.com/RenewableEnergy/RenewableEnergyHome

Read about renewable energy in the United States at:

www.eia.gov/energyexplained/index.php?page=renewable_home

For more information on energy and how we use it, check out:

online.kidsdiscover.com/unit/energy?ReturnUrl=/unit/energy

Publisher's note to educators and parents:
Our editors have carefully reviewed these websites to ensure that they are suitable for students. Many websites change frequently, however, and we cannot guarantee that a site's future contents will continue to meet our high standards of quality and educational value. Be advised that students should be closely supervised whenever they access the Internet.

Index